OPUS 1

Progression in Music 11–14

Steve Block
Karen Brock
Chris Hiscock
Derek Hobbs
Peter Roadknight

Editor: Steve Block

www.heinemann.co.uk

✓ Free online support
✓ Useful weblinks
✓ 24 hour online ordering

01865 888058

Heinemann is an imprint of Pearson Education Limited, a company incorporated in England and Wales, having its registered office at Edinburgh Gate, Harlow, Essex, CM20 2JE. Registered company number: 872828

Heinemann is the registered trademark of Pearson Education Limited

© Pearson Education Limited, 2006

First published 2006

10 09 08 07
10 9 8 7 6 5 4 3

British Library Cataloguing in Publication Data is available from the British Library on request.

ISBN: 978 0 435812 08 9

Copyright notice

Printed in China by South China Printing Company

Produced by Artistix

Cover photo: © ImageState

Picture research by Jemma Street and Natalie Gray

Acknowledgements

The author and publisher would like to thank the following individuals and organisations for permission to reproduce photographs:

Biblioteca Medicea-Laurenziana, Florence, Italy/ The Bridgeman Art Library p.26 (bottom); Carey Brandon/ Redferns p.8; Chris Stock/Lebrecht p.49; Corbis p.19; Daniel Aubry , Odyssey Productions, Chicago p.48 (all); Darrell Gulin/Corbis p.46; Dk/Alamy p.49; Lebrecht Music & Arts/Alamy pp.21, 36 (bottom), 39, 44, 49, 5; Getty Images/PhotoDisc pp.19 (left, second left and second right); iStockphoto/Nathan Jones p.12; Kunsthistorisches Museum, Vienna, Austria/ The Bridgeman Art Library p.26 (top); Musee Marmottan, Paris, France/ Giraudon/ The Bridgeman Art Library p.54 (both); Musiko-Musikaa pp.16 (both), 17; Odile Noel / Redferns p.49; © Pictorial Press/Alamy p.15; Phil Dent/Redferns p.25; Philip Ryalls / Redferns p.36 (top); Tim Mosenfelder/Corbis p.6; Uppsala University Library p.52; Worldwide Picture Library / Alamy p.34; Yani Yordanova / Redferns p.30.

The publishers would also like to thank the following for permissions to reproduce lyrics and/or music:

Music by Oasis on pages 5 and 7 from:
The Importance Of Being Idle
Words & Music by Noel Gallagher
© Copyright 2005 Oasis Music (GB).
Sony/ATV Music Publishing (UK) Limited.
Used by permission of Music Sales Limited.
All Rights Reserved. International Copyright Secured.

Lyrics by Polly Paulusma p.8
© Sony/ATV Songs LLC. All Rights Reserved

Music and lyrics to 'Somewhere', p.11 © Copyright 1959 by the Estate of Leonard Bernstein & Stephen Sondheim. Copyright Renewed. Leonard Bernstein Music Publishing Company LLC, Publisher. Boosey & Hawkes, Inc., Sole Agent. INTERNATIONAL COPYRIGHT SECURED.

Lyrics to 'One Note Samba', p.20
One Note Samba (Samba De Uma Nota)
Words by Newton Mendonca
Music by Antonio Carlos Jobim
© Copyright 1961, 1962 & 1964 Duchess Music Corporation, USA.
Universal/MCA Music Limited.
Used by permission of Music Sales Limited.
All Rights Reserved. International Copyright Secured.

Every effort has been made to contact copyright holders of material reproduced in this book. Any omissions will be rectified in subsequent printings if notice is given to the publishers.

Contents

Unit 1	What makes a good song?	4
1.1	Good songs need a rocking riff	5
1.2	Good songs need a sturdy structure	6
1.3	Good songs need luminous lyrics	8
1.4	Good songs need a memorable melody	10
1.5/1.6	Songwriter's sketchpad	12

Unit 2	Latin beat	14
2.1	Music in Latin America	15
2.2	Rhythms in Andean music	17
2.3	The music of Brazil	19
2.4	The music of Villa-Lobos	21
2.5/2.6	Composing an Amazonian scene	23

Unit 3	The folk tradition	24
3.1	What is folk music?	25
3.2	What are modes?	26
3.3	Changes and differences	28
3.4	Folk accompaniments	30
3.5/3.6	Arranging a folk melody	32

Unit 4	Rhythms of the Nile	33
4.1	How are cyclic rhythms used in Egyptian music?	34
4.2	How are call and response rhythms used in Egyptian music?	36
4.3	Performing 'Halawaya'	38
4.4	Egyptian music looks west	40
4.5/4.6	Egyptian composition	42

Unit 5	Medieval music	43
5.1	What was music like in medieval times?	44
5.2	What is parallel motion?	46
5.3	Discovering more medieval instruments	48
5.4	More on medieval church music	50
5.5/5.6	Medieval influences on more recent music – including your own!	52

Unit 6	Impressionism	53
6.1	What is Impressionism?	54
6.2	How did Debussy use scales?	56
6.3	How did Debussy create descriptive effects?	58
6.4	More impressionist techniques	59
6.5/6.6	Composing your own impressionist piece	61

Glossary		63

What makes a good song?

In this unit you will:

- recognise and explore how riffs fit into a song
- describe the structure of a song using appropriate musical vocabulary
- identify and explore the relationship between music and lyrics in a song
- describe and evaluate melody in a song
- get to know songs from a variety of genres, including rock, jazz and stage musical

by:

- listening to and analysing how songs are put together
- performing key parts of songs vocally and with instruments
- composing a riff, melody and lyrics for your own song

because:

- riffs are an important feature of songs
- the structure of songs helps to keep an audience's attention
- lyrics reflect the structure and carry the meaning of the song
- melody is the most memorable part of a song.

Good songs need a rocking riff

In this lesson you will:

- recognise how riffs fit into a song
- learn how to perform a riff from simple notation

- decide what makes a great band.

'Riffs' in rock songs

'The Importance of Being Idle' was a top ten single by Oasis. Like many successful rock songs, it begins with a memorable **riff**. Riffs are normally made of just a few notes, arranged in a pattern and repeated. They get the song off to a great start by providing a simple, memorable idea which catches the listener's attention. A riff is similar to an **ostinato** (repeated pattern), but a riff tends to be used on and off in a song, whereas an ostinato is usually more continuous.

'When the time comes to sit down and do the writing, ideas are the support system of a song. Without them, lyrics, tunes, and arrangements mean nothing … Make sure you have a basic concept that excites you and justifies all the hard work.' (Joel Hirschhorn, whose songs have sold almost 100 million records, taken from *The Complete Idiot's Guide to Songwriting*)

Listening and performing

1 You are now going to listen to and perform the riff from 'The Importance of Being Idle' using instruments.

  a Listen to the **introduction** of the song and then clap out the rhythm of the riff.

  b Listen to the riff again, following the 'full riff' part on the score below. The riff lasts for four bars. Which three bars are the same and which are different?

  c Now have a go at performing the riff using instruments. If you're working on a keyboard, play with your right hand and do not forget the G sharp in the last bar. You may find it easier to start with the 'simple riff' part.

  d Listen to your classmates play the riff and appraise their performances.
- Did they play the correct notes, including the G sharp?
- Could you feel a steady beat in the music?

2 Lead singer of Oasis, Noel Gallagher, once said 'We are the biggest band in Britain of all time, ever'. What do you think about this statement? What other bands could make the same claim? What makes a great band?

Good songs need a sturdy structure

In this lesson you will:

- explore the structure of a song using appropriate musical vocabulary

- learn how to maintain your own part in a group performance.

Oasis's first album, *Definitely Maybe*, became the fastest-selling debut in British history and their 1995 release, *(What's The Story) Morning Glory?* has sold more copies in Britain than any of The Beatles' albums.

Members of Oasis have often been in the news for their frequent disagreements with each other and the media. So how have Oasis succeeded in writing chart-topping rock songs for more than a decade?

When writing a new song, the composer needs to make important decisions about its **structure**.

- How will the song start and finish?
- Will the song include an **instrumental**?
- How many **verses** will be included?
- How long will the whole song last?

The effectiveness of the structure will depend on getting the balance of the various sections just right.

The band Oasis

Listening to and performing 'The Importance of Being Idle'

1 The previous lesson focused on a riff from the introduction of 'The Importance of Being Idle'. Now listen to the whole recording to work out how the song is put together. As you listen, identify the different sections of the song. Use the information in this grid to help you.

Section name	Features
Chorus (or **refrain**)	Focal point or climax of the song. **Lyrics** are usually the same each time, often containing the song title.
Verse (or strophe)	Alternates with the chorus in a song. Tells 'the story', or narrative, of the song. There are usually 2–3 verses in a song.
Instrumental	Has no singing, just instruments. Provides a change from the singing.
Bridge (or pre-chorus)	Links the verse and the chorus. Not all songs include a bridge.
Middle 8	Contrasting vocal **section**. Usually appears only once, towards the middle of a song.
Introduction	Opening section of the song. Normally instrumental.

Playing

2 You have already practised a riff from 'The Importance of Being Idle' in the previous lesson. Continue to work on this part or rehearse the chords or bass line parts below, which make up the introduction. Once you have practised your part, work in groups of four and produce an ensemble performance of the music. Each member of the group should play a different part.

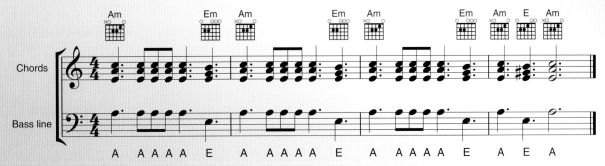

3 Now listen to your classmates play the riffs and appraise their performance. For each performance identify:
- one thing that they did well
- one thing that they could aim to improve next time they perform.

Do the same for your own performance too!

Good songs need luminous lyrics

In this lesson you will:

- identify and explore the relationship between music and lyrics

- learn about the role of the hook and the outro in songs
- begin writing your own song lyrics.

Polly Paulusma

About lyrics

One thing that makes songs distinct from instrumental music is, of course, the use of words. Song words are known as lyrics. The word 'lyric' comes from Ancient Greece, where songs were often accompanied by a small harp called a lyre (just as today's songs may be accompanied by a guitar). The lyrics of a song usually tell a story or convey a message, and often express the singer's feelings about something or someone.

Listening to 'Dark Side'

1 Almost as important as the content of the lyrics is the way they are organised. Listen to 'Dark Side' by Polly Paulusma to find out how the lyrics are structured in this song. As you listen, follow the song timeline below.

| 0:17 min | 0:49 | 1:16 | 1:48 | 2:07 | 2:33 | 3:05 | 3:27 |

| | 'Come and ask me if I want to dance with you / I think you will ...' | ''Cause I've danced with romeos and gigolos, philosophers and slackers ...' | 'I was thinking love was just a complicated game / you play in the dark ...' | ''Cause I've danced with romeos and gigolos, philosophers and slackers ...' | 'Now that you've warmed me / I never want to be that cold again ...' | 'Take my hand and lead me where the music is alive ...' | ''Cause I've danced with romeos and gigolos, philosophers and slackers ...' | 'No they've never shone on the dark side of my moon ...' |

Identify which colour represents which section of the song – chorus, verse, introduction, ending and middle 8. Here are three clues to help you and some questions to consider about song structure.

- The chorus always has the same lyrics and the same music. *(Why would a composer want the chorus to be repeated several times in the same song?)*
- The lyrics of the chorus usually contain the title of the song. *(Why might it be better to take the song title from the chorus, rather than from one of the verses?)*
- The lyrics change for each verse, though the music remains the same. *(Why do songwriters write a number of different verses for a song?)*

Structure of a song

The hook

When listening to any song, listen out for the **hook** in the chorus. This is the phrase that catches your attention and its words are usually used for the song's title. Think of Beatles' songs such as 'Help!', 'A Hard Day's Night' or 'She Loves You'. What hooks can you think of from today's songs?

The outro

The ending, or final section, of a song is known as the **outro** – a made-up word meaning the opposite of 'intro' (introduction). It can also be called the **coda**.

2 Listen to the outro of Polly Paulusma's 'Dark Side' and compare it to the outro of Oasis's 'The Importance of Being Idle'. In what ways are the endings similar and different? In what other ways can songwriters finish songs?

3 Finally, write some lyrics for a verse and chorus of your own song. You can use them when you get a chance to write your own song later. Be sure to write a strong, memorable hook into your line 1, line 4 or both.

Good songs need a memorable melody

About melody

Where have you been? How many different ways can you ask that question? Listen to the sound of your voice. Does the **pitch** go up or down? Does it move up and down in steps or are there some jumps in pitch? Which words are drawn out and which are short?

Every time you talk, the pitch of your voice will rise and fall to add expression to your words. In music, too, melodies move up and down, sometimes in steps and sometimes in sudden leaps. And, like speech, melodies have their own **rhythm** to keep our interest.

About *West Side Story*

The 1957 Broadway musical *West Side Story* is a retelling of Shakespeare's *Romeo and Juliet*. Set in the slums of New York, two rivals gangs called the Jets and the Sharks take on each other in a fierce battle. Caught in the middle of this gang warfare is the love story of Tony (a former Jet) and Maria (sister of Bernardo, the Sharks' leader). While attempting to stop a fight, Tony inadvertently kills Bernardo. Tony makes his way to Maria's home and finds her mourning her brother's death, although she is comforted by seeing Tony. The two lovers console one another as Maria sings the well-known song 'Somewhere' – but the Sharks want revenge. The stage is set for the story's thrilling climax.

Listening to 'Somewhere'

1 Do you know the story of Romeo and Juliet? What happens at the end of this Shakespeare tragedy? And how is the ending changed in the *West Side Story* version? See if you can find out.

2 Listen out for when Maria sings the words printed in the score below. Do you think this melody suits the story of Tony and Maria? Why? Which parts of the melody do you think are most effective? Which parts stick in your memory? Are the music and lyrics well matched?

3 Now listen again to the verse and follow the score. Can you hear and see which words the following features come on:
- the highest note
- the lowest note
- a large leap in pitch
- several shorter notes
- several long notes
- a series of steps upwards in pitch.

4 Now listen carefully to the three notes sung on the words *'place for us'* in bar 2 on the score (marked with an 'x'). They make a particular pitch and rhythm pattern. There are at least three more places in the whole melody where this pattern is sung to different words, and sometimes on a different starting note. Try to find these places. (It is repetition like this that helps to make a melody more memorable.)

Singing

5 Practise singing 'Somewhere' with the class. Concentrate on developing your vocal technique and expression.

Songwriter's sketchpad

In this lesson you will:

- create a riff and melodies for the verse and chorus of your own new song
- build on previously composed song lyrics

- prepare a performance of your new song
- appraise your own song, and the songs of others in the class.

Some musicians take years to write a handful of songs, whereas others seem to be able to compose more freely. The German composer Franz Schubert (1797–1828) wrote up to eight songs a day. In his short life, he composed more than 600 songs!

Writing your own song

To write your own song, you need to combine the four main elements: riff, structure, lyrics and **melody**. You should have composed the lyrics for a verse and chorus earlier in this unit. You will need these for this lesson.

Use the following simple structure, which you can extend later:
- intro, using riff
- verse, including lyrics
- chorus, including lyrics
- outro, using riff.

1 Writing the chorus melody

- It's best to do this first, as the chorus needs to be the most memorable section. Practise chanting the words of your chorus, reminding yourself of the lyrics' natural rhythm and pulse,
- Now find the words of the hook. This is probably the same as your song title and you might have written it into Line 1 or 4 of your chorus lyrics. Choose a pattern of notes that will make the hook even more memorable. Sing it over several times to make sure it works.
- Now write the melody for the rest of your chorus. Remember repeated shapes or patterns, memorability/catchiness, variety of pitch/movement/rhythm, expressive blending of lyrics and notes. You can alter any part (tune or lyrics) at any time. This is how songwriters normally work.
- Stick to a few notes. (Try using just A, C, D, E and G.)

- Don't pitch your melody too low – the chorus should be the high point of the song.
- Don't let your melody 'jump around' in pitch too much, or it will be harder to remember.
- Use an interesting rhythm, but make sure it fits with the lyrics.

2 Writing the verse melody

- Practise chanting the words to feel their natural rhythms.
- Make sure the verse melody does not outshine the chorus melody. Pitch the notes of the verse melody a little lower than the chorus, using a smaller range of notes and introducing some repetition.
- Now, practise putting the verse and chorus together. Make any improvements you think necessary.

3 Riff

The instrumental riff will form the intro and outro of your song.
- Stick to a few notes, e.g. A, C, D, E and G.
- Aim for an 8-note riff. If you want, compose four notes and then repeat this pattern.
- Use mainly steps and small leaps between notes.
- Keep the rhythm of your riff simple. You could make all notes the same length.
- Keep it catchy and short.

4 Accompaniment

You could accompany your song with a rhythmic backing, e.g. an automatic rhythm on a keyboard. If you have time to experiment, or if you know how to use chords, you could use some of these chords: C chord (notes C, E, G), A minor chord (notes A, C, E), F chord (notes F, A, C) and G chord (notes G, B, D).

5 Performance

- Use different instruments and voices to perform the riff and the melody.
- Experiment with the way you play the riff (try playing it at the same time as your chorus).
- Organise the group so that some of you drop out and join in at different points.

6 Appraisal

Finally, listen to everyone else's work and think about how well their songs work. Do the same for your own song. Remember that you are appraising the quality of the song writing rather than its performance. Ask yourself these quesitons:
- Did it contain all the required elements: intro, outro, riff, verse and chorus?
- Did the chorus have a strong, memorable hook? (Can you still remember it now?)
- Did the melody and lyrics work well together?
- Was repetition used, and was it effective?
- What was the overall impact of the song? How could it be improved?

Latin beat

In this unit you will:

- learn about the instruments and rhythms used in the music of the Andes
- perform an Andean-inspired piece using simple rhythms, ostinatos and melodies
- learn about the music of Brazil and play bossa nova
- listen to the music of a South American composer
- use some of the features you have learnt about to create your own Amazonian scene

by:

- listening to typical Andean instruments in the piece 'Leño Verde' and performing simple Andean rhythms
- listening to typical pieces from different areas of Latin America
- performing and composing bossa nova rhythms
- learning about the music of Brazilian composer Villa-Lobos and listening to two of his orchestral pieces, 'The Little Train of the Caipira' and 'Forest Fire'

because:

- Latin American styles have had a big influence on other types of music, and continue to do so
- different types of Latin American music have distinctive sounds.

Music in Latin America

In this lesson you will:

- learn something of the history and context of Latin and South American music

- begin to recognise some of the characteristic instruments and sounds of Andean music.

Music of the Andes

The oldest musical tradition in **Latin America** is that of the native Indians who live in the **Andean** mountains. Most of their instruments date from ancient times and include panpipes, flutes, guitars, harps and drums.

Spanish and Portuguese invaders in the sixteenth century brought with them their own songs and dances. These became mixed with the native Indian styles. Later on, slaves transported from Africa brought with them their own very rhythmic styles. This unique mixture led to the Latin styles that we know today. They include:

- the **tango** dances of Argentina and Uruguay
- the **bossa nova** and **samba** carnival music of **Brazil**
- the exciting rhythms of the **salsa** and **rumba** of Cuba.

Latin pop has been hugely successful in recent years. Many major recording artists have released Latin hits – for example, Madonna's 'La Isla Bonita' and Lou Bega's reworking of 'Mambo No. 5'. There have been Latin remixes by Britney Spears, Will Smith and Jamiroquai among others, and there are Latino stars such as Enrique Inglesis, Jennifer Lopez and Ricky Martin. None of this could have happened without the influences of the music you will learn about in this unit.

Instruments of the Andes

Panpipes are ancient instruments, which have been found on Inca and Aztec carvings. The hollow pipes are made of various lengths of bamboo, each producing a different pitched note, and the instruments themselves come in various sizes. A sound is made by blowing across the top of the hollow pipes.

Playing the panpipes

The **charango** is a version of the European mandolin-type instruments brought by the Spanish settlers. 'Charango' means 'armadillo' in the Quechua language. The body of the charango used to be made from an armadillo shell, because there was a shortage of wood in the Andes.

> Modern versions of the charango are made of wood. What possible reasons can you think of for this change?

Listening to 'Leño Verde'

Leño Verde is Spanish for 'green wood'. It is a Latin American piece. Listen out for the panpipes and the charango.

1 Which instruments begin the piece?

2 The music is divided into three main sections:

    (1) the panpipe enters, with each phrase echoed by a second panpipe

    (2) the first panpipe plays the main melody, repeated by a second panpipe

    (3) the first panpipe plays a simple three-note theme, echoed by the second.

3 Listen to the two panpipes in Section 1. They seem to copy each other. Do they play exactly the same notes? How are they similar and how are they different?

4 Here are three graphic musical shapes of the beginning of each main section. Which graphic shape (**A**, **B** or **C**) belongs to which section (**1**, **2** or **3**) of the music?

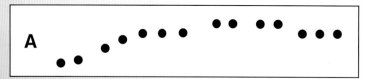

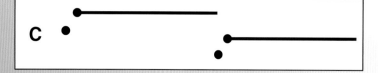

5 How does the piece end?

Rhythms in Andean Music

In this lesson you will:

- get to know various rhythms, ostinatos and melodies related to Andean music, some of them using syncopation

- learn about another traditional Andean instrument – the **bombo**.

Listening to *'Floreo de Llamas'*

'Floreo de Llamas', meaning 'Dance of the Flames', is a popular Andean piece. The piece has four beats in every bar ($\frac{4}{4}$) and is in the key of E minor, which needs F♯. Here are the four pitched accompaniment patterns. They are all played together and keep repeating until the end of the piece.

In many Andean pieces there is an accompanying rhythm played by the *bombo* (a deep Andean drum). What natural materials do you suppose the traditional *bombo* is made from? What man-made materials might be used in modern *bombos*?

Here are the melodies. 'A' is the main melody (tune) of the piece, which is played after an introduction and returns again after the middle section. It features a **syncopated** rhythm.

Melody 'B' is the melody of the middle section, which has the same syncopated rhythm.

Note that the order in which these two melodies are played – A B A – produces a structure that we call **ternary**.

The piece begins with an **ostinato** (repeated pattern) on a deep drum, to sound like the Andean *bombo*. This is played throughout the whole piece. The words might help you to remember the rhythm.

R1

E - cua - dor, E - cua - dor.

Here are two more ostinato rhythms, with supporting words, which could be added on suitable untuned percussion instruments.

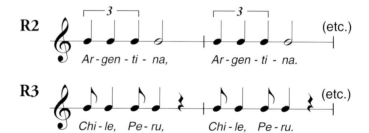

R2

Ar - gen - ti - na, Ar - gen - ti - na.

R3

Chi - le, Pe - ru, Chi - le, Pe - ru.

Performing *'Floreo de Llamas'*

Work together in small groups.
1 Practise playing the four pitched accompaniments, P1, P2, P3 and P4.
2 Now, using untuned percussion instruments, practise the ostinato R1. Think about what instruments would be most suitable for this piece of music. Once you can play this, have a go at playing the other ostinatos or create one of your own.
3 Now play the melody.
4 Finally, put all the parts together to make a really good performance. What do we mean when we talk about a 'really good performance'? How would it apply to this piece in particular?

The music of Brazil

In this lesson you will:

- learn something about the music of Brazil, and about the bossa nova in particular

- learn about bossa nova rhythms and harmonies, and experience the texture they create when combined.

Brazilian music is some of the most varied in South America. The exciting carnival sounds of the samba and the jazzy bossa nova are known across the world. Both styles originated in the city of Rio de Janerio on the east coast of Brazil.

What is bossa nova?

The Brazilian style of dance music called bossa nova developed from the more percussive samba. The Spanish name 'bossa nova' can be translated as 'new wave', 'new trend', 'new way' or even 'new beat'. The Brazilian songwriter Antonio Carlos Jobim first developed bossa nova in the 1950s and 60s and used it in some of his most famous songs such as 'The Girl from Ipanema' and 'One Note Samba'.

Cabasa, claves, guiro and maracas – some common Latin American untuned percussion instruments

Performing a bossa nova rhythm

Use the four rhythms A, B, C and D on page 20 to create a typical bossa nova backing. Repeat the rhythms over and over, like an ostinato. You could start by clapping them, then use untuned percussion to make the backing sound more Brazilian.

Try this combination for the four rhythms.

- **Part A:**   Edge of small drum (like a 'rim-shot')
- **Part B:**   Cabasa or other shaker
- **Part C:**   Bass drum or other large drum
- **Part D:**   Claves

The words shown in Part **D** should help you to clap or play the rhythm more accurately.

'One Note Samba' (Samba de Uma Nota So)

Antonio Carlos Jobim's famous bossa nova is called 'One Note Samba'. However, it is not a Samba and it has more than one note!

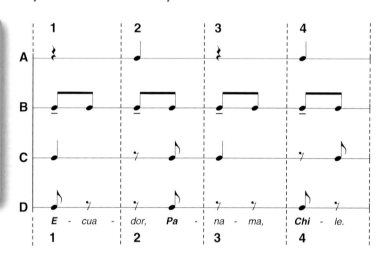

Listening to 'One Note Samba'   10 & 11

1 How many different notes are there in the main melody?

2 When you have heard the piece through, start to learn how to sing the melody to the words below. The rhythm is jazzy and syncopated, but the pitch is very easy.

This is just a little samba built upon a single note,
Other notes are bound to follow but the root is still that note.
Now the new one is the consequence of the one we've just been through,
As I'm bound to be the unavoidable consequence of you.

3 How does the composer get away with writing a melody with just two different notes in it? (Think about what else is in the music.)

4 Now listen to a different performance of 'One Note Samba' by American jazz musician Stan Getz. Listen out for as many similarities and differences as you can between the two versions you have heard today.

The music of Villa-Lobos

In this lesson you will:

- learn more about the music of Brazil and about the composer **Villa-Lobos**
- find out more about Latin American percussion instruments

- explore syncopated rhythms.

Heitor Villa-Lobos (1887–1959) is one of Brazil's best-known composers. He had no formal music education and was mainly self-taught. He often travelled around Brazil researching its folk music. He believed that Brazilian music should have its own national flavour, and he made use of the folk music and instruments of Brazil in his own music.

Villa-Lobos was particularly clever at using percussion instruments to create a musical picture. One of his best loved pieces is 'The Little Train of the Caipira'.

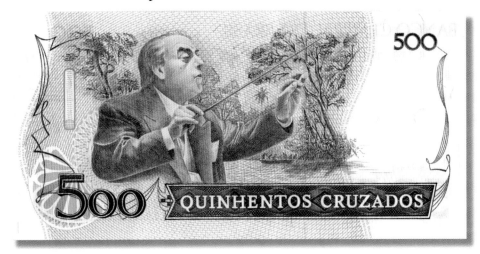

Villa-Lobos appears on a Brazilian banknote. A famous English composer appears on a British banknote. Find out which composer and which banknote.

Listening to 'The Little Train of the Caipira'

Caipira (pronounced '*kye-peera*') was a nickname given to migrant workers on the fruit plantations in the Brazilian hills. Villa-Lobos apparently wrote this piece while he was riding on a steam engine that took *caipira* to work. Picture the little train as a rickety old thing that takes a while to build up steam and get moving, especially as the track must have had a long incline (slope) to reach the hilly areas.

Once the engine reaches 'full steam ahead', it keeps going for a while and we can settle into the journey. Halfway through, however, the music suddenly changes – use your imagination as to what has happened here. Finally, the train pulls into the station with a great deal of noise and then, as if totally exhausted, it gradually grinds to a halt (listen for the high-pitched squealing of the brakes on the metal wheels) and releases its excess steam.

Villa-Lobos makes particular use of Latin American percussion in this piece and this is one of the reasons why the piece sounds so Brazilian. Another reason is the use of typical Brazilian rhythms, which often feature syncopation.

1 How does Villa Lobos use instruments to create the following effects? **15**
   • The engine building up steam.
   • The train leaving the station.
   • The train slowing down to enter the station.
   • The engine letting off steam.
2 How does the piece end?
3 Look at the diagram below. The top line of music is an unsyncopated version of the rhythm that is heard in the main melody of 'The Little Train of the Caipira'. Clap this rhythm. In the lower version (which is how Villa-Lobos actually wrote it), you can see by the red lines how the syncopation is made by the notes sounding earlier.

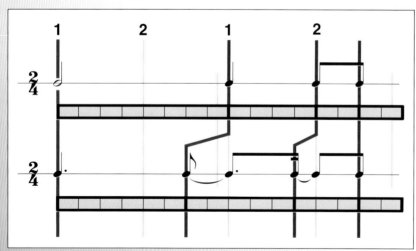

4 Listen again to 'The Little Train of the Caipira'. How many times does this syncopated rhythm feature in the main melody?

Composing an Amazonian scene

In this lesson you will:

- review the features of Latin American music that you have learnt about so far
- use some of these features to create your own Latin-influenced piece.

You are going to work together to create your own 'Amazonian Scene'. Each group will compose a short piece that will combine with others to make one big scene. Your composition should be no more than three minutes long. There will be two distinct sections – A and B.

Step 1   Choose one of these titles for your piece:
1 Mountain Journey – descent to the Amazon
2 Amazon River Journey
3 Amazon Jungle Journey
4 Amazon Rainforest Journey

Include all the following features:
- one or more Latin-sounding ostinato patterns (rhythmic or melodic)
- a main melody, with some syncopation
- Latin percussion sounds
- ternary form (A B A) (see page 18).

Step 2   Look back through this unit at some of the **rhythm** patterns, **scales**, **chords** and **melodies** used in **Latin** American music. Choose some to include in your piece. You can always adapt them if you need to.

Step 3   List the sounds you want to imitate and events you want to portray for your chosen title. Organise them into two groups – one for Section A and one for Section B. You might want one or two ideas to appear in both sections or continue throughout the piece.

Step 4   Discuss which ideas you want to use and how you will use them. Which fit your chosen sounds/events? What instrument will you use, or could you use your voices? Should you change the ideas or use them as they are? Which ones will work well together? You might want to introduce some ideas of your own – you can be as imaginative as you like!

Step 5   Organise your ideas into Sections A and B. Consider these points as you work.
- Think about the general mood you want to create and decide on a suitable tempo.
- When creating your melody, begin with an ostinato pattern and fit the melody to this.
- Be clear about what differences there will be between Sections A and B.

Step 6   Think carefully about how your piece will begin (the introduction) and how it will end. Finally, practise your piece and make changes if necessary. Remember, the aim is to create an Amazonian scene that has a real Latin American feel to it.

The folk tradition

In this unit you will:

- learn about British folk music and its function in society
- understand how it is passed on and how it still plays a part in popular music
- learn about musical modes and scales and how they are used in folk music
- consider some of the ways in which performers/arrangers create new versions of folk melodies
- learn how folk melodies can be accompanied and make a musical arrangement of your own.

by:

- exploring various modes, scales and melodies, and the intervals used in them
- getting to know two British folk songs, 'Scarborough Fair' and 'Drunken Sailor', by singing, playing and arranging them
- comparing and contrasting several more folk songs and their musical features
- using drones and chords
- performing your arrangement and appraising your own and others' work

because:

- folk music is a key part of our musical heritage and has played such an important part in society
- folk music has an enduring popularity and continues to influence other types of music
- you can apply your understanding of folk music, drones, chords and arranging techniques to create arrangements of your own.

What is folk music?

In this lesson you will:

- learn something about British **folk music**
- learn how the pentatonic scale works and how it is used in folk melodies.

Some tunes that are still known today are hundreds of years old. Many were made up by people who had not been taught how to read and write. Their songs were passed on from memory to other people. Each time a person learnt a new song they might, either deliberately or accidentally, change the tune or some of the words. Folk songs are still performed and listened to today by many people, both in their traditional form and in modern folk styles such as **folk rock**.

A folk festival

What are scales?

A scale is a series of pitched notes arranged in order of height, from which melodies and harmonies can be made. A **mode** is very similar and sometimes the two words are used to mean the same thing. The particular notes chosen for any scale will make a huge difference to the sound of the music using that scale, and **composers** will choose carefully to give their music a special 'flavour'.

1 Folk rock often uses electronic instruments, modern harmonies and rock **rhythms** to accompany old folk tunes. Can this be classed as 'folk music'?

The pentatonic scale

Many folk songs from around the world are based on the **pentatonic scale**. In **pentatonic melodies** just five different pitches are used (*penta-tonic* = 'five notes'). The pentatonic scale is quite easy to work with because these notes will usually fit together in any order or combination.

Listening

17 & 18

2 Listen to two British pentatonic folk melodies, both from Scotland. The first is the 'Skye Boat Song', about the escape of Bonnie Prince Charlie to the island of Skye after his defeat at the Battle of Culloden in 1746. The second is 'Auld Lang Syne', which means 'times of long ago'. What do you think each song might best be used for (a–d), and why?

a A march to battle   **b** A lullaby   **c** A work song   **d** A celebration song

What are modes?

In this lesson you will:

- learn about two musical modes, Dorian and Ionian, and how they are used in folk music

- learn about two popular British folk songs.

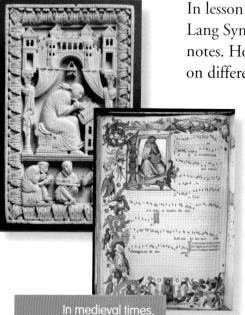

In lesson 3.1 you learned that many folk melodies, such as 'Auld Lang Syne', are pentatonic. They are built on just five different notes. However, there are many other folk melodies that are based on different modes.

In the Middle Ages, church leaders in Europe decided to arrange the many Christian chants – early hymns – into categories using a system of 'modes'. Each mode had its own particular 'flavour', according to the layout of **tones** and **semitones**.

The modes were named after areas of ancient Greece, because the church leaders believed they were copying the principles of ancient Greek music. So the church modes have names such as **Ionian**, **Dorian**, and **Phrygian**.

In medieval times, monks often wrote music

Exploring modes

1 • Play up and down a C major scale. The C major scale is made up of the eight white notes on a piano or keyboard from C to C. Listen to the sound of the first and last notes (both Cs). They feel like 'home notes', where the music can finish comfortably. This is why the first and last notes of the scale have the same name (C in this case).

- Now play the scale from D to D, again using white notes only. These are the notes used in the Dorian mode. How is the 'flavour' of the scale different? Do the first and last notes (both Ds) still feel like **home notes**?

- You can start on any white note and do the same. Each time you do so you will produce a different mode. Even the scale we call 'C Major' is actually the Ionian mode on C!
The keyboard on page 27 shows the notes of the Ionian and Dorian modes shown on a keyboard. Notice how the semitones come between notes 3–4 and 7–8 in the Ionian/**Major** mode, but between 2–3 and 6–7 in the **Dorian mode** – hence the different sound or 'flavour' of each mode.

However, it's important to remember that **modal** melodies do not have to stay within the range of eight notes that you have been playing. For example, in 'Scarborough Fair' and 'Drunken Sailor' (see below) the tunes dip below the bottom printed note of the scale. Also, many melodies will start on a different note of the mode, but still keep the flavour of the mode.

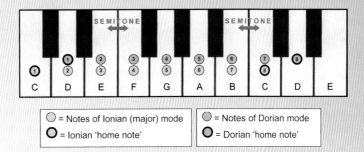

Listening

19 & 20

2 Listen to two traditional English folk songs, which you may recognise, 'Scarborough Fair' and 'Drunken Sailor'. Both are in the Dorian mode. As you follow the **melody** line and first **verse** of each, remember that performers will usually change the notes or rhythms of folk songs to suit their own style and taste – just as in pop, rock and jazz. Sometimes even the words change!

Scarborough Fair

Drunken Sailor

3 Now sing the two songs yourselves, either with the recordings or with another accompaniment.

Changes and differences

In this lesson you will:

- begin to understand change and development in folk music

- learn more about British folk songs
- learn more about certain modes and scales.

1 You have probably heard or learned about evolution in nature. Try to think of connections between evolution and the history of folk music.

Music has never really 'stood still'. It has always developed and changed – sometimes gradually over time, sometimes very suddenly. Some of the changes happen unintentionally or unavoidably; others are deliberate choices. Here are some of the reasons why a piece of music might be changed to sound quite different. How intentional might each change have been? How gradual or sudden might such a change be? Might the change become permanent?

- A rock singer makes a 'cover' version of a song from last year's charts.
- The original melody of a folk song is lost, only the **lyrics** survive.
- A modern orchestra records a piece originally written for 'ancient' instruments.
- A folk singer performs a song in a different mode because it sounds sadder that way.
- A traveller likes a song that she hears being sung in a small village inn, so she tries to teach it to friends a few days later.
- A rapper includes a well-known classical tune in one of his new songs.

2 Now listen to extracts from three different British folk songs. The graphic scores on page 29 show the first part of each song, but the scores are not in the same order as on the CD. As you listen, decide which score fits which extract.  **21, 22 & 23**

3 Look look at the notes used in each song and decide which scale or mode is used: pentatonic, major (Ionian) or Dorian. (Don't worry if one or two notes of the scale or mode aren't used in the melody.)

Folk song 1

					F								
				E			E	E					
			D	D					D	D			
											C		
												B	
	A	A											

Folk song 2

	C	C	C	C		C							
					B								
									F				
								E		E			
											D		
C												C	C

Folk song 3

			E								
				D							
		C			C						
									A		
G					G		G		G		
						E		E			
										C	

4 Sing the opening phrases of Folk song 1 and 2 to get the feel of the scale or mode that each song uses.

5 The following instruments were used in the extracts – **melodeon, guitar, strings, fiddle** (violin) – but which were used in which extract?

Mode swap

6 a Work out the phrases of Folk songs 1 and 2 on an instrument taking care to play the notes at the correct pitch.

b Again using Folk songs 1 and 2, swap the modes for the major (Ionian) tune and the Dorian tune. Move all the major tune notes UP a step to put them in the Dorian, and all the Dorian tune notes DOWN a step to put them into the major. Remember to stay on the white notes all the time. What difference does this make to the way the tune sounds?

Folk accompaniments

In this lesson you will:

- learn about some of the ways in which folk melodies can be accompanied

- begin to make musical **arrangements** of your own.

Some of the folk songs you have already heard in this unit have been sung **a cappella** (without accompanying instruments). However, most have had some form of instrumental backing or **accompaniment**. Those accompaniments had to be worked out by the musicians who performed them or by an **arranger**. Changing or adding an accompaniment is one of the most effective ways of arranging and performing a folk song.

Kathryn Tickell playing the Northumbrian pipes

Drones

A **drone** is a continuous pitched note sounding through the music. It may be a very long note or a pattern of repeated notes but it is always at the same **pitch**. Sometimes the drone can have *two* pitches played together. A drone is often played on the 1st or 5th notes of the scale, or even both together, and it is usually played below the melody. The drone is one of the simplest ways to add another layer to a melody.

A number of folk instruments are capable of providing their own drone, e.g. the **Northumbrian pipes** (a type of bagpipes, but smaller).

1 Listen to two instrumental versions of the folk tune 'Small Coals and Little Money'. **24 & 25**
   Both versions are performed on the Northumbrian pipes. In both, the drone starts before
   the melody and continues throughout the whole piece.
   a Which version uses a drone on *one* pitch? Which uses *two* pitches?
   b In which version does the drone change from sustained notes to repeated rhythmic notes?
   c Which version has another instrument providing a strong rhythmic accompaniment as well? What
      instrument is it?
   d Which version has a more 'authentic' feel to it, and which sounds like a more modern
      arrangement? What features of the music tell you this?
2 You can produce a drone very easily yourself by humming a long note while someone else sings a
   tune over the top. Try this now with 'Scarborough Fair' (see page 27), holding on to the first note of the
   tune. If possible, try to take your breaths at the end of each phrase.

Chords

One of the versions of 'Small Coals', which you just listened to, not
only had a drone that accompanied the melody, it also had **chords**.
A chord is a group of two or more pitched notes played at the same
time. The **effect** of any chords in a piece of music will depend on
the choice of notes, as well as the way the chords are played. For
example, what effect do the chords have in 'Small Coals'?

3 You can add **harmony** to 'Drunken Sailor' (see page 27) by using just
   two chords:
   D minor chord (Dm)   = D + F + A
   C major chord (C)   = C + E + G
   Concentrate on the chorus first and work out which chord fits each
   part of the tune.

Drones and chords: when
used together, they do
not have to fit all the time.
For example, a D drone
might be heard against a
C chord.

Arranging a folk melody

In this lesson you will:

- learn about some of the ways in which performers and arrangers create new versions of folk melodies

- bring together the things that you have learned in this unit.

Listening to modern arrangements of folk tunes

Earlier in this unit you learned how music can change and develop over time. Performers and arrangers can make folk melodies sound more modern by altering or adding instruments, harmonies and so on. Why do you think that performers and arrangers feel the need to create new versions of old folk melodies?

1 Listen to the folk song 'All Around My Hat', which is sung in two contrasting versions. The first is by folk singer Andrew Scarhar and the second is an arrangement by the group Steeleye Span. What differences can you identify between Scarhar's version and Steeleye Span's?

Making your own arrangement of a folk tune

2 To make a modern arrangement of an old folk tune, 'Drunken Sailor', first choose a title that will help you to set the mood of your arrangement: 'The Sailor's Funeral'; 'The Sailor's Wedding'; or 'The Sailor's Disco'. Alternatively, use a title of your own.

3 Once you have decided on your title and agreed the mood of your arrangement, think about how you will include the following features:

   a the 'Drunken Sailor' melody (altered to suit the new mood), sung, or played or both

   b a drone (one-note or two-notes, sustained or rhythmic)

   c chords, for example, C and Dm

   d at least one verse and chorus of the song

   e an introduction and an ending (usually called a **coda**).

   How will each feature be used to achieve the mood you want? How will you fit the different ideas (melody, drone, chords, verse/chorus, introduction/coda) together to produce the best effect? You can review and refine your plan as you go along – this is how most composers and arrangers tend to work.

4 When your arrangement is complete, perform and record it. Then use your appraisal skills to make a critical, constructive evaluation of your own and others' work.

Rhythms of the Nile

In this unit you will:

- learn about different types of instruments and rhythms used in Egyptian music
- understand how music is used in Egyptian society
- discover how Egyptian music can be linked to music of other cultures

by:

- listening to, performing and composing traditional rhythms in Egyptian music
- listening to and appraising the use of Egyptian instruments
- listening to and performing an Egyptian wedding dance, *'Halawaya'*
- comparing modern music from the USA, and listening to Western classical music influenced by Egyptian music
- bringing together what you have learned in the unit to create your own group composition

because:

- learning about Egyptian instruments will help you to recognise the distinctive sounds of Egyptian music
- learning about Egyptian music will help you appreciate the ways in which music may be used in society
- the rhythms used in traditional Egyptian music have influenced music of other cultures
- understanding the links between Egyptian music and music of other cultures will help you understand how they share similarities as well as differences.

How are cyclic rhythms used in Egyptian music?

In this lesson you will:

- learn something of the history and context of Egyptian music

- begin to recognise some of the characteristic instruments and sounds of Egyptian music.

Egypt is located in the north of Africa

Egypt is a country in North Africa. The continent of Africa is famous for its rich musical culture, particularly its drumming and singing traditions. Drums have been used over many centuries to accompany dancing and singing, and to communicate from one village to another. **Rhythm** is a key feature of African music and the roots of many Western musical styles, such as jazz, rock and pop, can be traced to the music of Africa.

Rhythm in Egyptian wedding music

Traditional music in Egypt and the Arab world is most often heard at special occasions such as parades and weddings. Typically at an Egyptian wedding a dancer leads the wedding couple into the reception room with their guests, accompanied by musicians chanting and playing rhythms on **percussion** instruments. The ceremony is a mark of prestige, and the dancer's role is to bless the wedding to bring good luck and prosperity.

An Egyptian wedding

1 How does the description of an Egyptian wedding compare with any wedding that you have been to or heard about? Are there any features in common?

'Halawaya' is a wedding chant and dance. It uses **cyclic** (**ostinato**) patterns which repeat or recur in cycles. After a while, these repetitions can produce an almost hypnotic effect on the listener. Whereas much Western music is 'linear' and designed to take the listener on a musical journey, cyclical music aims to take the listener 'out of time'.

Listening to *'Halawaya'*

2 Listen to *'Halawaya'* performed by musicians from the Nile. How does the music make you feel? What instruments can you hear? Discuss your thoughts with a partner.

Performing an Egyptian ostinato rhythm

You are now going to learn a typical Egyptian ostinato rhythm. The rhythm is made up of two parts – A and B as shown below. Part A can be played on any hand drum using either one or two hands. Part B could be played on any other untuned percussion instrument.

3 **a** Play Part A using two hand strokes – a heavier stroke in the centre of the drum and a lighter stroke on the rim (edge of skin). The combination of these two strokes will create variety to the sound, and add interesting stress patterns to the rhythm.

b Repeat the rhythms over and over again to create a longer **section** of music – this makes the rhythm into an **ostinato**, and the music becomes **cyclic**. We can use this repeated rhythm as the first section of a new piece.

4 Now extend your drumming piece further by creating a contrasting second section. To recreate this scenario, use:

a in the background, a dramatic drum roll using rapid fingers movements (move to the centre if you want to increase the volume)

b in the foreground, sudden rhythmic 'messages' between either a leader and individual pupils, or between pairs or groups of pupils in the class. Make these up as you go along (this is called **improvisation**).

How are call and response rhythms used in Egyptian music?

In this lesson you will:

- learn about some more Egyptian instruments
- learn about **call and response** rhythms in Egyptian music

- review the meaning of **syncopation** and explore how syncopated rhythms feature in Egyptian music.

Call and response is when one person plays or sings a musical phrase and then another person (or group) responds with a different phrase or copies the first one. This can be between two traditional Egyptian drums like the ones described below.

The *dohol* being played with sticks

The dohol

The *dohol* (or *dohl* or *dohola*) is a double-ended hand drum traditionally used at weddings across Arabic countries and the Indian subcontinent. It has a bass head on one side and a treble head on the other and may be played by hand or with sticks, depending on the country and tradition.

The derbouka

The *derbouka* (or *derbuka*, *darbuka* or even *darabuka*) is a goblet-shaped drum with the skin tightly fixed over the wide end. The tightness of the skin gives the derbouka a high, slightly tinny tone. The *derbouka* is played with either the fingers or the flat of the hand giving a variety of strokes which produce many different sounds.

The *derbouka* drum

1 Why do some Arabian or Indian instruments have several different spellings in English?

Listening to *'Zahrafat al as'id'*

2 First listen to an extract from *'Zahrafat al as'id'* (Rejoicing in Upper Egypt), which will help you to identify the different sounds of the dohol and the derbouka. Now listen to a second extract from the same piece. This extract is performed by two Egyptian drummers playing the dohol and derbouka and it has two sections. After you have listened to the second extract, select two descriptions from the list below to match the music of the two sections in the extract. Remember: **improvising** is making music up as you go along.

  A Improvised rhythms played on the derbouka, over a slow ostinato rhythm played on the dohol.

  B Call and response rhythms passed between the derbouka and dohol.

  C Solo improvisation on the derbouka alone.

  D Both the derbouka and dohol playing the same ostinato rhythm together.

Composing

3 a Now use what you have learnt in this lesson to extend your drumming piece from lesson 4.1. Create a new contrasting section by improvising an unbroken sequence of call and response rhythms between leader and individuals. This can be accompanied by a small group of drums playing either a steady **pulse** or the following ostinato rhythm:

Opposite is a chart showing the different sections of your piece so far.

b Now agree on an effective **structure** (i.e. organisation of sections) and perform your drumming piece as a class.

> **MAIN IDEA** Rhythms A+B *(from Lesson 4.1)*
>
> ⬇ ⬇
>
> **CONTRASTING IDEA** Rhythmic messages over drum rolls *(from Lesson 4.1)*
>
> ⬇ ⬇
>
> **CONTRASTING IDEA** Call and response sequence over pulse or ostinato rhythm *(from this lesson)*

More about syncopation

One feature of *'Halawaya'* is **syncopation** (see Unit 2, pages 17–18). Syncopation is a way of changing a rhythm by making some notes sound as though they are being played early. They cross over the main beat of the music. Syncopated rhythms and **melodies** are a characteristic of Egyptian music. Look at the notation below, taken from another Egyptian piece called *'Ansam'*.

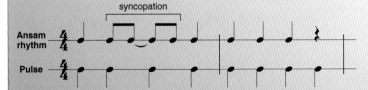

4 Divide into two groups or pairs. One group should clap the *'Ansam'* rhythm and the other group should clap the pulse (beat). Can you feel the 'tension' between the syncopation and the beat? What effect does this have?

Performing *'Halawaya'*

In this lesson you will:

- learn more about how melodies and rhythms are improvised in Egyptian music

- take part in a class version of an Egyptian piece.

Listening

28

1 a Listen to the *'Halawaya'* extract again and follow this score of the voice and clapping parts:

b Compare the voice melody at the beginning and when it repeats. How is the repeated version different? Watch out for this difference as you learn the melody.

c The clapping pattern is tricky, as it does not do what you expect it to. Use this rhythm grid to practise it.

1	2	**3**	4	**1**	**2**	**3**	**4**	**1**	2	3	**4**	1	2	**3**	4

...*shub* | *bah*

1	2	3	**4**	1	2	**3**	4	1	2	**3**	4	**1**	**2**	3	**4**

d Here is another rhythm grid showing the cyclic percussion parts that you can use to accompany the melody and clapping parts (the instruments are just suggestions):

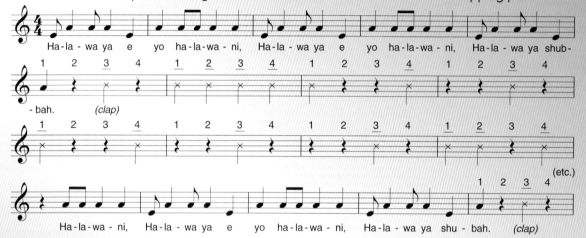

	1	2	3	4	1	2	3	4
Large drum	•							
Medium drum	•			•	•			
Small drum			•				•	•
Cowbell							••	•
Shaker	••	••	••	••	••	••	••	••

Improvising during 'Halawaya'

Remember that improvising is making music up as you go along. On the recording of 'Halawaya' you can hear (a) rhythmic improvisation on drums and (b) melodic improvisation on an oud. The oud is a plucked stringed instrument similar to the European lute.

2 a To add to your own 'Halawaya' piece, improvise your own drum rhythms during the clapping section that separates each repetition of the chant.

b Now improvise a two-note melody over the drum accompaniment, using one of the following pairs of notes: (i) E and A; (ii) C and E.

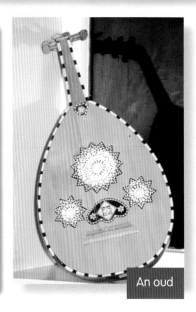

An oud

Performing

Finally, here is one possible structure for your whole class performance of 'Halawaya':

	Section 1	Section 2	Section 3	Section 4	Section 5
Vocal chant + clapping	✓		✓		✓
Percussion rhythms	✓	✓	✓	✓	✓
Rhythmic improvisations during the clapping section only	✓		✓		✓
Melodic improvisations		✓		✓	

3 a Which sections have the same **texture**? (Remember that 'texture' describes the layers of sound that combine to make the music.)

b How many different textures are there?

c If each section with a different texture was given a letter (A, B, etc.), which of the following would represent the overall structure in letters?

A B C D E   A A B C C   A B A B A   A B B A B

Egyptian music looks west

In this lesson you will:

- learn how Egyptian music has influenced, and been influenced by, the music of other cultures

- understand the difference between a Western and an Arabic scale
- learn how a **drone** can be used in music.

Historically, Egypt has had strong trading links with Arab countries, the Far East, Africa and Europe. As a result many musical traditions have passed between the Western world and countries such as Egypt. Egyptian music making has also been influenced by Arab culture, particularly in the use of Arabic scales such as the *Maqam Hijaz* scale.

The importance of scales

Notes in a scale can be different musical distances, or **intervals**, from each other. Most are either a half step (**semitone**) or a whole step (**tone**) apart from each other, as in the Western C major scale shown below. But in many Arabic scales there might be a bigger step (worth three semitones) and more half steps, giving the scale and the music a very non-Western sound.

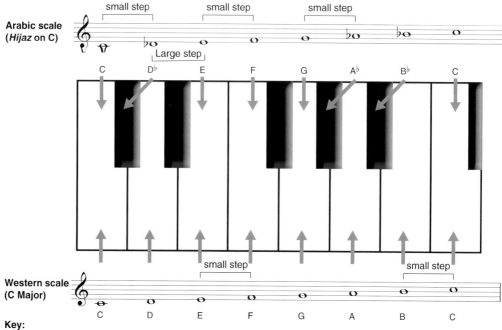

Key:
Small step: semitone
Large step: 3 semitones

Listening

1 On page 40, the Western major scale and the Arabic *Maqim Hijaz* are shown against a music keyboard. See if you can work out the differences between them. Listen to the Western major scale and the Arabic *Maqim Hijaz* being played. Now play them yourself.

Playing drones

In traditional Arabic/Egyptian music, a **drone** is usually the only kind of **harmony** that is used. It is a continuous pitched note sounding through the music (see page 30). It might be a very long note or a pattern of repeated notes, but it is always on the same **pitch**. Sometimes the drone can have *two* pitches played together. Often a drone is played on the 1st or 5th notes of the **scale**, or even both together.

2 **a** Play the C major scale over a <u>C drone</u>. Now play it over a <u>G drone</u>. Finally play it over <u>both C and G together</u>. Do the same with Maqam Hijaz. How does the drone change the music?

  b Now play the drone note/s low down, and then up high instead.

Listening to Egyptian influences on Western music

3 Listen to an extract from the opera *Aida* by Giuseppe Verdi. It was written in 1871 for Cairo's new opera house, which had been built to celebrate the opening of the Suez Canal two years earlier. Now listen to film composer Bernard Hermann's opening music for the 1954 epic film *The Egyptian*. Listen out for the sound of the **Arabic scales** and the **drones** that the composers introduce above or below the melodies. What other features of the music contribute to the Egyptian sound?

Listening to Western influences on Egyptian music

Many contemporary Egyptian composers have successfully blended Arab scales, vocal styles, vocal improvisation, drones and **unison** melodies with Western instruments and harmonies creating exciting new rhythms, textures and forms.

4 Listen to an extract from a contemporary pop song: Britney Spears' 'Toxic':

  a Identify any traditional Egyptian features and Western features that appear in the song.

  b Why do you think musicians include ideas from other cultures in their music?

  c Can you think of any other music that you listen to that is influenced by the music of another culture?

Egyptian composition

In this lesson you will:

- put together what you have learned in this unit to create your own group composition.

You are going to work with a group to compose a piece built around what you have learned in this unit about traditional Egyptian music.

Composing on Egyptian piece

Select a title from the following:
- Camel train
- Nile journey
- Desert oasis.

Alternatively, come up with your own title.

Features

Your composition should include each of the following ideas, to help illustrate the title you have chosen.
- An unaccompanied, freely improvised melody: use the notes of the *Maqam Hijaz* scale (see page 40).
- A syncopated ostinato drum rhythm (for example to describe any movement suggested by the title).
- A drone using the 1st and/or 5th notes of the *Maqam Hijaz* scale (for example to create a background 'wash' of sound).
- A melody to fit with the drum ostinato – either use just the 1st, 5th or 8th notes of the *Maqam Hijaz* scale or use the first five notes of the *Maqam Hijaz* scale.

Extension ideas

- Additional drum rhythms – combine with your syncopated rhythm.
- An 8- or 16-beat clapping pattern – combine with your drum rhythm/s.

Medieval music

In this unit you will learn:

- about the times in which medieval music was developed and how a medieval piece would have been performed
- about the instruments used in medieval times and the sounds they made
- about some of the ways in which medieval songs were accompanied
- that the church influenced how music was written and performed

by:

- learning about influences on medieval music
- listening to and performing examples of English and French medieval music.
- learning about typical musical devices of medieval music, such as plainsong, parallel motion and melisma
- learning how medieval music has influenced contemporary composers
- composing your own piece using medieval devices

because:

- you will be able to recognise medieval music and understand how musical ideas flourished in an age of change
- a wide variety of styles of simple accompaniments such as ostinato, drone and call and response can be used in music
- understanding how medieval musicians composed pieces, for example by using plainsong and parallel motion will develop your knowledge of compositional techniques.

What was music like in medieval times?

In this lesson you will:

- learn something about the medieval period, its music and the influence of the Middle East
- listen to a piece of thirteenth-century dance music

- review two features of medieval music: **drone** and **ostinato**.

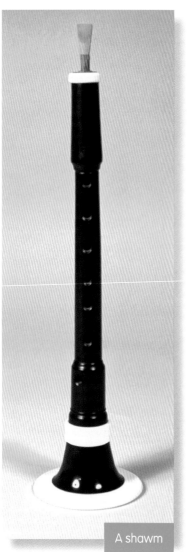

A shawm

The medieval period spanned from about the time of the Norman invasion of England in 1066 to the crowning of the Tudor king, Henry VII, in 1485. 'Medi-eval' actually means 'Middle Ages' – another popular term for the period. It was a time of great change and conflict. Not only were there many Crusades to the Holy Land, but also England fought a long war with the French and the country fell into civil war during the Wars of the Roses.

It was also a time of change for music. New musical ideas were developed by monks and nuns in the monasteries. Minstrels, or troubadours, travelled throughout Europe entertaining royal courts as well as the ordinary people with their singing. Their songs were often stories of love, heroism and bravery or tales from olden times. Thanks to the work of the monks and nuns, music was beginning to be written down in a way that we would recognise today.

Influences from the Middle East

The Crusades were a series of wars that aimed to free Jerusalem from the Arab Saracens. All the armies of Christian Europe united, and kings, knights and soldiers travelled to the Holy Land to fight. On their return they often brought back instruments from the East, such as the guitar-like *oud* (see Unit 4: Rhythms of the Nile) and the shawm, which was a wind instrument similar to the modern oboe. When the Saracens sent soldiers into battle, shawms were played to add to the terrifying noise of the approaching army, in the same way that the Scots used bagpipes.

'La Quinte Estampie Real' ('The Fifth Royal Estampie Real')

The *Estampie* was a popular type of dance in the thirteenth century and, from pictures of the time, it involved stamping or hopping. Similar movements can be found in Turkish dances today, showing its Middle Eastern origins. The French *'La Quinte Estampie Real'* features the shawm accompanied by high and low drums.

Listening to 'La Quinte Estampie Real'

37

1 a Listen to the drum accompaniment at the beginning. Match what you hear with one of the **rhythm** patterns opposite:

b Does the rhythm pattern stay the same throughout the extract?

c Now tap the pattern lightly on your lap – you could tap one leg for the high drum and the other for the low drum.

2 If the *Estampie* was a stamping dance, why do you think this music would be suitable for it?

3 a How would you describe the sound of the shawm?

b Why do you think the shawm was used by the Saracens for playing on the battlefield?

c What instrument would *you* use to frighten your enemies?

Reviewing drone and ostinato

Two features commonly found in medieval music are the drone and the ostinato. The drone is a continuous very long note (or notes) or pattern of repeated notes, which is always the same **pitch** and sounds throughout a piece of music. The ostinato is a short **melody** or rhythm that is repeated over and over again.

Performing

4 a Working with a partner, choose one person to perform a drone and the other to perform an ostinato.

b Spend about five minutes composing a very short piece that demonstrates what a drone sounds like when combined with an ostinato.

c Now compose a second short piece that still demonstrates the drone and ostinato correctly but sounds different to the first piece – change parts for this one.

d Now choose one of your pieces and perform it to the class.

What is parallel motion?

In this lesson you will:

- learn about parallel motion and its use in medieval music
- sing and play a thirteenth-century sacred song from France, using parallel motion, drone and ostinato
- listen to a modern **arrangement** of the same song.

Parallel railway tracks

At the start of the Middle Ages music sometimes consisted of a melody line with little or no **accompaniment**. When there is only one line of notes, the **texture** is referred to as monophonic (from the Greek for 'one sound'). Listen to an example of a monophonic chant and follow the notes on the score below:

39

A - - le - - - - lu - ia.

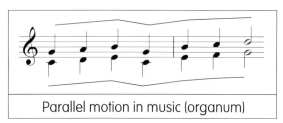
Parallel motion in music (organum)

Though this very pure sound has survived for over a thousand years, medieval music often also uses a device called parallel motion to add simple **harmony** to the melody line. You are probably familiar with the mathematical concept of 'parallel lines', (lines which are always the same distance apart). The same can occur in music. Parallel musical lines can change direction and still stay the same distance apart, just like railway tracks.

In medieval music the addition of a second parallel part was called organum. This technique gradually led **composers** to write more complicated harmonies to accompany melodies.

Singing

1 Create your own organum by pairing up with someone to sing or play the beginning of a well-known tune such as the 'EastEnders' theme or *'Frère Jacques'*. Each of you should start on a different note. Try it with one person starting on the note C, and the other on the note G (above or below). What **effect** does this parallel motion have on the sound of the music?

Singing and playing 'Salva Nos'

Salva Nos ('Save us') is a piece of thirteenth-century music from France. It celebrates the Virgin Mary as the saviour of mankind. We do not know exactly how and where it was performed, but sacred songs were popular with minstrels and monks alike.

You are going to put together a performance of *'Salva Nos'*, using some of the devices you have learned about: drone, ostinato and parallel motion. The melody is in the **Dorian mode** (see pages 26–27). The Latin words in Melody A: *'Salva nos stella maris et regina celorum'* mean 'Save us, star of the sea and queen of heaven'.

2 a First practise the Latin words.

b Then, sing the words to Melody A, which is sung four times throughout:

c Once you are confident with this melody, play it on a tuned instrument.

d Here are the other parts that you will need when you put the piece together.
Melody B should be played on tuned instruments. This has a lower part added in parallel motion:

The ostinato and drone parts should be played on tuned instruments, tambourine and drum, throughout.

Discovering more medieval instruments

In this lesson you will:

- learn more about instruments used in the Middle Ages

- put together the parts you have learned for 'Salva Nos' and perform the piece as a class.

Shawm
Loud wind instrument with a double reed (often inside the top of the instrument).

Hurdy gurdy
Box-shaped instrument with strings. Turning the handle scrapes a wheel gently against the strings, playing drone and melody.

The rebec
Small-bodied instrument with a neck and strings. It is bowed and fingered like a violin.

The psaltery
Strings stretched across a triangular wooden sound-box are plucked like a harp.

Lute
Plucked instrument with a large pear-shaped body. Held and played like a guitar.

Although there are no recordings of the original medieval instruments, we know quite a lot about them from medieval manuscripts and paintings, and from a few surviving instruments. Below you will see five pictures taken from a very famous illuminated manuscript in Spain called the *Cantigas de Santa Maria*. There are also five photos of modern reproductions (copies) of the same types of instrument in the manuscript. There are a number of 'early music' experts who make and play these instruments today.

Manuscript A

Manuscript B

Manuscript C

Manuscript D

1 Read through the names and descriptions for the five medieval instruments in the pictures and photos. Match each instrument name and description with the correct manuscript picture and reproduction photo.

Listening

37, 42, 43, 44

2 Listen to four short recordings of medieval dance music, including *'La Quinte Estampie Real'*, which you have already heard. Using the descriptions above, match the instrument combinations (a–d below) with the correct extract number (1–4).

a Rebec, psaltery and harp   **c** Shawm and drums

b Lute and voice   **d** Psaltery and hurdy gurdy

Performing *'Salva Nos'*

3 In the previous lesson, you worked on the melodies, drone and ostinatos for *'Salva Nos'*. Now put them all together and perform it to the class.

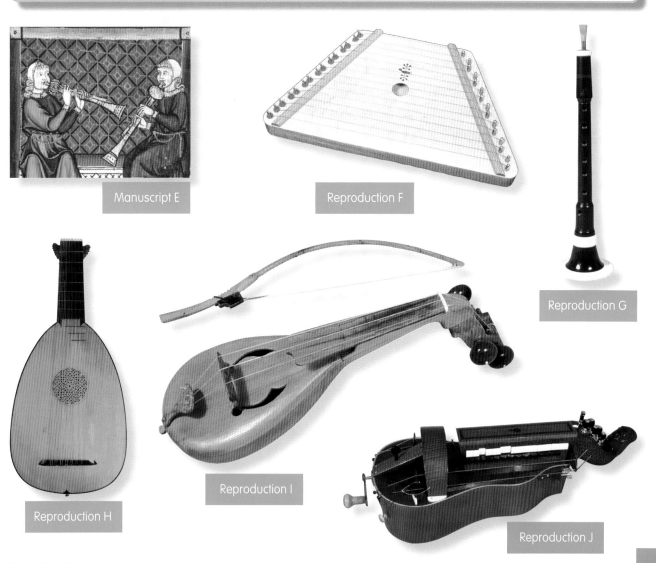

Manuscript E

Reproduction F

Reproduction G

Reproduction H

Reproduction I

Reproduction J

More on medieval church music

In this lesson you will:

- learn about plainsong and melisma, and create your own versions of these

- learn more about parallel motion.

Plainsong and melisma

Plainsong was first developed by early Christians who set simple prayers or psalms to music. It did not have any accompaniment. Plainsong is also known as Plainchant or Gregorian Chant (after the sixth-century Pope Gregory who is said to have influenced its spread through Europe). This monophonic music has appeared on many recordings of 'music for relaxation' in recent years. Many listeners feel it has a timeless, almost hypnotic, effect on them.

Listening

Listen again to the 'Alleluia' track that you heard in lesson 5.2: What is parallel motion? (page 46). Can you feel that effect at all?

Here is the melody for the first part of the 'Alleluia'. Notice how the four syllables of the word 'all-le-lu-ia' are stretched across 15 notes. When a string of notes is sung to one syllable, it is called a melisma.

Vocal improvising

1 **Improvise** your own plainsong using one of the four-syllable phrases below. Don't forget to include at least one melisma:

'Good afternoon'   'What's for dinner?'   'Have a nice day!'

Sing it to a partner, and ask them to sing an answer back to you in 'plainsong'.

Developing parallel motion: intervals

Parallel motion in music (organum)

You already know that medieval music often uses parallel motion to add simple harmony to a melody line. You also know that parallel musical lines can change direction but still stay the same distance apart.

In the example shown above, the two lines of notes are described as a '5th apart'. The 5th is an **interval**, or musical distance, between the notes. We have looked a little at intervals in previous units, but you need to understand how they are measured.

To measure the interval between any two notes you must count from one to the other in steps, *always remembering to include the two notes themselves.*

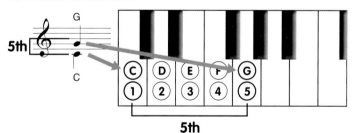

So, on the keyboard above the notes C and G are a 5th apart (C-D-E-F-G : 1-2-3-4-5). The notes C and F are a 4th apart, C and E are a 3rd apart, and from C to D is a 2nd.

---

2 How far is it from D to F? And from D to G? What is the interval between E and G?

Of course, you can measure an interval downwards in exactly the same way as upwards. So, if a 5th above C is G, a 5th below G is C!

3 Practise playing the following phrase on a glockenspiel or keyboard. Now add a parallel part underneath at each of the intervals shown below:

G   A   B   C   D

a a 5th below

b a 4th below

c a 3rd below.

Which version/s do you think sound most medieval? Explain your answer.

Medieval influences on more recent music - including your own!

In this lesson you will:

- compose your own 'medieval' piece, using what you have learned in this unit.

Composing

Medieval melodies and composing techniques have continued to be used by musicians long after the Middle Ages. Now you have an opportunity to put together some of the musical devices and techniques that you have learnt about in this unit. As the basis of your composition you can use part of the melody of the twelfth-century 'Hymn to St Magnus'.

Here is the first part of the St Magnus melody:

The original manuscript of the 'Hymn to St Magnus'

Include all of the following features in your piece:

- ternary form (Section A – Section B – Section A)
- the St Magnus melody as the main tune in Section A
- a new melody for Section B, using notes from the Dorian mode

- parallel motion in 3rds, 4ths or 5ths with one of the melodies
- a drone using either D and A or A and E
- one or more ostinato patterns repeated all the way through

Add a brief **introduction** and **coda** to your piece to finish it off (this could be just the drone and ostinato patterns).

Once you have composed your piece, give it a suitable title. Rehearse and record your piece. Then listen to the pieces of others in the class and appraise their work and your own.

Impressionism

In this unit you will learn:

- about impressionist music and the important use of timbre
- about the work of an important impressionist composer, Debussy, and his use of scales, chords and chord clusters to create descriptive effect
- how to follow and create a graphic score
- how other composers are influenced by impressionist music

by:

- listening to, performing and composing impressionist music
- focusing on the work of Debussy and his descriptive pieces
- following and creating your own graphic scores
- listening to music by Vaughan Williams

because:

- timbre is a crucial characteristic in impressionist music
- the use of scales and chords will help you understand music
- using graphic scores will broaden your knowledge and understanding of different notation
- looking at the influence of impressionism will help you understand how groups of composers can share a common approach.

What is Impressionism?

In this lesson you will:

- identify common characteristics in impressionist art and music by listening to impressionist pieces and relating them to impressionist paintings

- reflect on characteristics of Debussy's impressionist music, in particular his use of **timbre** (tone colour) and unusual **melody**
- listen to Debussy's *'Nuages'*, focusing on the timbre, the instruments and the melodies.

Impressionist art

The word 'Impressionism' is used to describe a style of painting developed by a group of French artists in the mid-nineteenth century. Impressionist painting is characterised by:

- the creation of a *general* impression of a scene or object rather than a photographic likeness
- using unmixed primary colours and small brush strokes to simulate real and reflected light.

Impressionist artists astonished everyone with their sensitivity towards colour and light. Today, impressionist paintings are among the best loved in the world. The most famous impressionist painters include Monet, Renoir, Pissarro and Manet.

Composers interpreted this new style of art in terms of music. Perhaps the most famous impressionist composer was the Frenchman Claude Debussy (1862–1918). Three characteristics of Debussy's music are:

Detail from Monet's 1872 painting *Impression, soleil levant* 'Impression, sunrise' showing impressionist brushstrokes

- sensitivity towards timbre (like the impressionist painters' sensitivity to colour)
- use of **scales** and **modes** from medieval and Far Eastern music
- use of chords to create descriptive effects.

Timbre is one of the main elements of music. It means the particular 'colour' of a sound. For example, a violin and a trumpet sound very different even when they play the same note – each has its own timbre or 'tone colour'.

Debussy's music caught on quickly. Soon there was a whole generation of composers who developed his impressionist ideas further. These included Ravel in France and Vaughan Williams, Delius and Holst in England.

Listening to 'Nuages'

'Nuages' is the first of a set of three pieces for orchestra composed by Debussy in 1899. 'Nuages' means clouds, and the piece describes the movement of clouds across the sky. In 'Nuages', Debussy carefully selects instrumental timbres (tone colours) from the orchestra to create different effects. His melodies have unusual shapes and his **accompaniments** often consist of either sustained, atmospheric **chords** or chords that follow the **rhythm** and shape of the melodies, moving in parallel motion.

1 Listen to three of the melodies from 'Nuages' and follow their graphic shapes below.

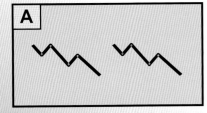 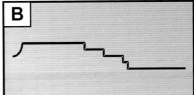 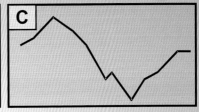

Debussy's use of instruments in 'Nuages' 50 & 51

2 a Listen to two extracts from 'Nuages'. The first is made up of four sections of music. The second is made up of three. Some of the sections vary in length. Some are quite short, some are longer. Each section begins with (and repeats) one of the three main melodies above.

   b Listen to the two extracts again and match the graphic shape (A, B or C) to the melody heard at the beginning of each section of music (seven sections in all).

3 In 'Nuage's, Debussy gives most of the melodies to the woodwind instruments of the orchestra. Match the melody heard at the beginning of each section to one (or more) of the following instruments: flute, oboe, cor anglais, clarinet, harp, violin.

4 How successful do you think Debussy has been in creating an impression of clouds in this piece?

How did Debussy use scales?

In this lesson you will:

- learn how Debussy used different scales to create moods and effects
- listen and respond to Debussy's piano piece *'Voiles'*
- find out how a whole tone scale works, and what its effect can be
- begin to learn a piece based on ideas from *'Voiles'*.

Debussy used different types of scales to give his melodies character and create particular moods or effects in his music. Some of his scales originate in Classical Western music, e.g. **major** and **minor** scales. Some he discovered in medieval music (e.g. modes), others he discovered in the gamelan music of Java and Bali (e.g. **pentatonic**). Debussy also explored new types of scale that had rarely been used before (e.g. the whole tone scale) and sometimes created his own scales.

1 Below are three scales that Debussy uses in *'Nuages'*. Play up and down each scale to get an idea of its sound. Can you hear how each scale has a character of its own?

2 With each scale or mode is an example of a melody from *'Nuages'* – you heard each of these in the previous lesson. Match them with the graphic shapes on page 55.

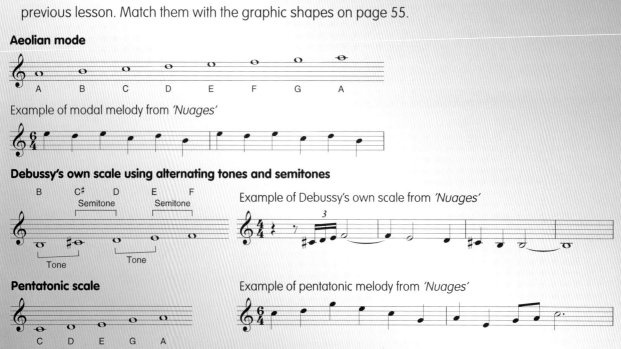

Aeolian mode

A B C D E F G A

Example of modal melody from *'Nuages'*

Debussy's own scale using alternating tones and semitones

B C♯ D E F
Semitone   Semitone
Tone   Tone

Example of Debussy's own scale from *'Nuages'*

Pentatonic scale

C D E G A

Example of pentatonic melody from *'Nuages'*

In 1889 Debussy attended an exhibition in Paris, where he heard the sound of the Javanese gamelan for the first time. The gamelan has a five-note (pentatonic) tuning called the slendro scale. Debussy was captivated by this sound and recreated it in some of his compositions. The pentatonic scale features in a great deal of his music.

A Javanese gamelan

The whole tone scale

Debussy's piano piece *'Voiles'* ('Sails') describes the movement of sailing boats on a calm sea. For this piece, Debussy uses a whole tone scale – see the example below:

All the notes in this scale are exactly the same **interval** apart (i.e. one tone), so it is hard to feel that any note sounds stronger or more like the 'home note' than any other. As a result, music made with whole tone scales often sounds dream-like and indefinite.

3 Play up and down the whole tone scale shown above to get an idea of its sound.

4 *'Hommage à Voiles'* ('Homage to *Voiles*') uses ideas from Debussy's *'Voiles'*: namely a whole tone melody that is shaped like the *'Voiles'* melody, and a rhythmic drone pattern. In addition, three ostinato parts make up the accompaniment. You are going to perform this piece as a whole class. Here are the parts:

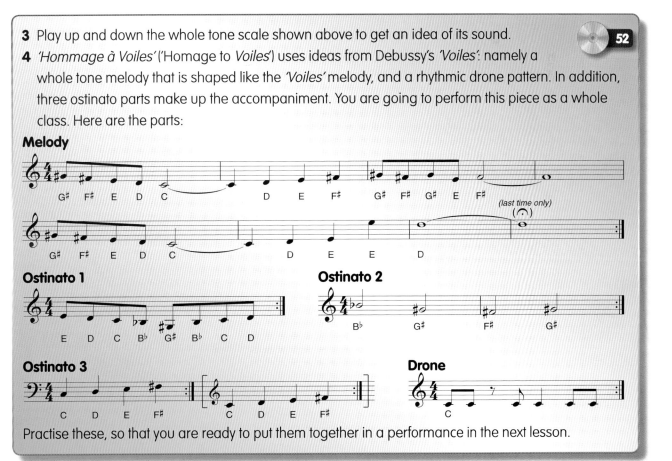

Practise these, so that you are ready to put them together in a performance in the next lesson.

How did Debussy create descriptive effects?

In this lesson you will:

- perform *'Hommage à Voiles'* and experience the effect of whole tone music

- learn how Debussy used descriptive effects in his piano music.

Throughout his life, Debussy composed many piano pieces. Many are short 'character' pieces with evocative titles. Listen to extracts from three of his piano pieces, each of which is meant to describe what it is called, and answer the questions below. The titles are: 'The snow is dancing', *'Canope'* (an ancient Egyptian burial urn) and *'Feux d'artifice'* (Fireworks).

1 a Match the beginning of each piece to one of the graphics opposite.

🔘 **53–5**

  b Select one musical element that you think features strongly in each piano piece: pitch; rhythm; timbre; texture; dynamics; structure; silence.

  c How does Debussy use your chosen element in each piece to help create what the titles suggest? Structure your answers as follows:
  I think that _____ is used effectively because…

  d Which piece do you think best suits its title, and why?

Performing *'Hommage à Voiles'*

2 a Revise the parts for *'Hommage à Voiles'* that you learned in the previous lesson.

  b Once you can play the parts together as a class, extend the piece by improvising 4- or 8-bar solos over the ostinato and drone accompaniment. For your solo improvisation you should use the notes of the whole tone scale. (Use either the same rhythm as the *'Hommage'* melody or a rhythm of your own.)

3 Alternate the *'Hommage'* melody with the improvised solo sections to create a rondo structure (A B A C A, etc.):

Section A	Section B	Section A	Section C	Section A
'Hommage' melody + accompaniment Dynamic: *mf*	Improvised solo/s + accompaniment Dynamic: *pp*	*'Hommage'* melody + accompaniment Dynamic: *mf*	Improvised solo/s + accompaniment Dynamic: *pp*	*'Hommage'* melody + accompaniment Dynamic: *mf*

More impressionist techniques

In this lesson you will:

- learn about chord spacing and clusters, and listen to their effect.

Creating atmosphere with chords and clusters

Impressionist composers use chords and clusters to create atmosphere and effects in their music. Below are four examples of ways in which they are often used.

1 Read the descriptions as you listen to examples 1–4:   **50, 51, 54, 55**

Chords	Effect	Example
Chord spacing	A chord can sound different according to the way that it is spaced. The spacing of a chord can make it feel deep, heavy, rich, light, harsh, bright, glowing, etc.	**1** *'Nuages'*: accompaniment to Melody B (see graphic shape on page 55)
Parallel chords	A sequence of chords played in parallel motion often produces a mysterious atmosphere.	**2** *'Canope'*: first section
Sustained chords	Chords or pairs of sustained chords can create a still, tranquil atmosphere or 'background wash'.	**3** *'Nuages'*: accompaniment to Melody C (see graphic shape on page 55)
Clusters	Clusters of two or three next door neighbour notes sounded together create a clashing effect that is often used descriptively.	**4** *'Fireworks'*: used to create the effect of exploding and jumping fireworks

Chord spacing

The spacing between chords creates different effects.

2 a Listen to the chord of A minor (A C E) using four different spacings and describe the feeling of each. Try these out for yourself on a keyboard instrument, as shown here:

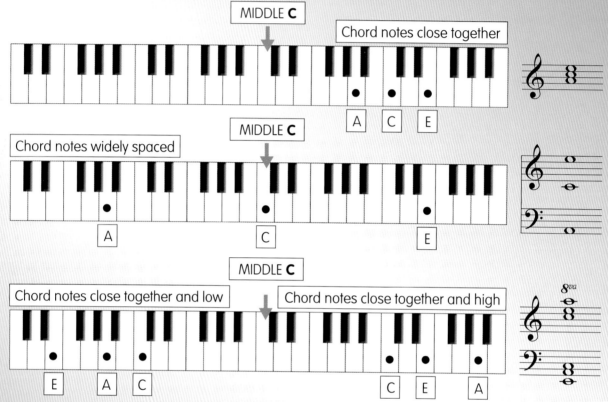

b In pairs or groups, find three different ways of spacing the D minor chord.

Clusters

Clusters are groups of adjacent notes sounded together. They are often used to create descriptive effects. Below are four clusters made up of adjacent notes from the pentatonic scale.

3 Play each one and listen to its effect.

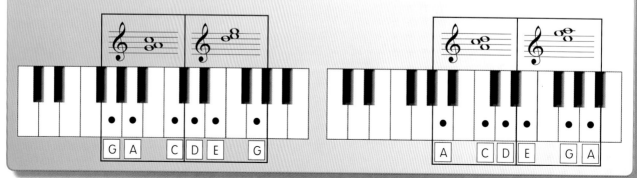

Composing your own impressionist piece

In this lesson you will:

- put together the impressionist techniques that you have learned in this unit, to compose an impressionist piece of your own

- appraise your own and others' work.

Composing

Compose a piece of music that creates the impression of one of the following: sunset; gymnastics; whale watching; space walk.

Structure

It might consist of either a single section or two or three contrasting sections of music. You could use ternary (A B A) or even rondo (A B A C A, etc.) structure – make sure that section A is your strongest, most memorable section. Make a plan using labelled boxes to show each section and what it will contain.

Scales

Either choose one of the following scales for your whole piece or use different scales for each contrasting section of your piece

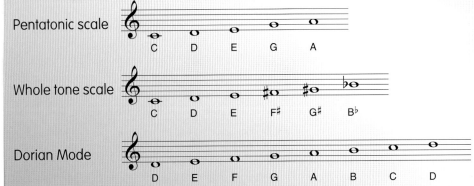

Impressionist composers often include some chromatic notes in their melodies, i.e. melody notes that move in semitone steps (e.g. C – C# – D are chromatic steps). You may choose to mix some chromatic notes in addition to the notes of your chosen scale.

Texture

Use the following:

- some parallel motion, e.g. two melodies that move in parallel motion or a series of parallel chords built on adjacent notes of the scale
- one or two widely spaced sustained chords built from notes of the scale you are using
- some clusters made up of three or four notes of the scale you are using.

Timbre

Choose instrumental and/or vocal sounds and combinations of sounds that you think are most appropriate for the effects and moods that you are trying to create.

Find a good way to notate your piece. You could use graphic symbols (like the ones used in earlier lessons), standard staff notation (five-line staves), or a mixture of the two.

Appraisal

When you've refined, rehearsed and recorded your composition, listen to your own and others' pieces and appraise them using these questions.

- Did the piece reflect its title? Was it a good 'impression'?
- What structure was used, and was it an effective way to organise the piece?
- What scale/s were used, and were they well chosen for the mood of the piece?
- Were parallel motion, widely spaced sustained chords and clusters all used? What effect did they have that reflected the title?
- Were the instruments/voices well chosen for their timbres, and did they help the mood of the music?
- Overall, was the piece effective and enjoyable?

A capella (p30) Refers to voices without an instrumental accompaniment.

Accompaniment (p30, 46, 55) Music that accompanies a melody line. The 'backing'.

Andean (p15) Coming from the Andes region of South America.

Andes (p15) Vast mountain range forming a continuous chain of highland along the western coast of South America.

Arrangement (p30, 46) Piece of music rewritten in a different way to the original, e.g. changing instrumentation, structure or mood.

Arranger (p30) A musician who makes an arrangement of a piece of music.

Bombo (p17) Deep Andean drum worn at the waist. Traditionally made from goatskin stretched over a wooden cylinder.

Bossa nova (p15) Brazilian style of dance music developed in the 1950s and 60s. Spanish for 'new wave', 'new trend', 'new way' or 'new beat'.

Brazil (p15) Largest and most populous country in Latin America. Capital is Brasilia; most famous city, Rio de Janerio.

Bridge/pre-chorus (p7) A transitional passage connecting a verse and a chorus.

Call and response (p36) One person plays or sings a musical phrase, then another person/ group responds with a different phrase or copies first one.

Charango (p16) Andean stringed instrument, plucked or strummed like a mandolin. Traditionally uses an armadillo shell for the instrument body.

Chord (p23, 31, 55) Group of two or more pitched notes played at the same time. The choice of notes determines the effect of the chord.

Chorus/refrain (p7) The part of a song that is repeated identically after each verse.

Coda (p9, 32, 52) Section that brings a piece of music to an end ((Italian for 'tail').

Composer (p25, 46) Musician who writes (composes) pieces of music.

Cyclic (p35) A melody or rhythm that is repeated over and over again.

Dorian (p26, 47) One of the modes used in music. Usually consists of 'white notes' from D to D.

Drone (p30, 40, 44) Continuous pitched note(s) sounding through the music. Very long note(s) or pattern of repeated notes, always same pitch. Most common drone notes are 1st and 5th notes of the scale.

Effect (p31, 46) The result or impact that music has on the person listening to it. Can also refer to a particular device, e.g. sound effect.

Fiddle (p29) The folk name for a violin.

Folk music (p25) Traditional 'music of the people', handed down over generations.

Folk rock (p25) Style containing elements of both folk music and rock music.

Guitar (p29) Popular stringed instrument, strummed or plucked. Usually has six strings. Can be acoustic or electric.

Harmony (p31, 41, 46) The effect produced by two or more pitched notes sounding at the same time. A chord creates harmony.

Hook (p9) A special musical phrase with lyrics, used in a song to catch the listener's attention and make them remember the song better.

Home note (p26) Term sometimes used to describe the main note of a key, mode or scale.

Interval (p40, 51, 57) A measure of the difference in pitch between two notes, e.g. semitone, tone, 3rd, 5th, etc.

Improvisation (p35, 50) Making up music as you go along, without preparation.

Instrumental (p6) An interlude in which there is no singing.

Intro/Introduction (p5, 52) The opening section of a song or piece of music. Comes before the first main section.

Ionian (p26) One of the modes used in music. Usually consists of 'white notes' from C to C. Sounds the same as the 'major' scale/ key.

Latin America (p15, 23) General name for the countries of Central and South America and some islands such as Cuba and Puerto Rico in the Caribbean.

Lyrics (p7, 28) The words of a song.

Major (p26, 56) Common Western scale or key. Semitones occur between notes 3–4 and 7–8, as in the Ionian mode.

Melodeon (p29) Folk instrument similar to accordion, with keyboard and bellows.

Melody (p12, 23, 27, 37, 45, 54)
A tune or succession of notes, varying in pitch, that have an organised and recognisable shape.

Middle 8 (p7) A section that breaks up the simple repetition of a verse/ chorus/verse/chorus structure by introducing new elements into the song.

Minor (p56) A type of mode, scale or chord sometimes used to convey a sadder mood (for example, D minor).

Mode (p25, 47, 54) A scale of notes from which melodies can be made. Each mode has a different structure of tones and semitones, giving it its own distinct 'flavour'.

Northumbrian pipes (p30) Set of bagpipes used in some folk music. Smaller and less strident than the Scottish (or Great Highland) pipes.

Ostinato (p5, 18, 35, 44) A repeated pattern. Can be rhythmic or melodic; usually short.

Outro (p9) The final section of a composition, which is added to give the song a satisfying conclusion.

Panpipes (p15) Ancient Andean instrument using hollow bamboo pipes of various lengths to produce different pitched notes when blown across.

Pentatonic (p25, 56) Pentatonic music uses a scale of just five different notes and is common in folk music (penta-tonic = 'five notes').

Percussion (p34) Instruments that are mostly hit, shaken or scraped to produce sound.

Pitch (p10, 30, 41, 45) Describes how high or low notes are.

Pulse (p37) A regular beat that is felt throughout much music.

Rhythm (p10, 23, 25, 34, 45, 55) A series of notes of different lengths that create a pattern. Usually fits with a regular beat or pulse.

Riff (p5) A repeated memorable idea, usually at or near the start of a song. Similar to a **ostinato**, but it tends to be used on and off rather than continuously.

Scale (p23, 25, 41, 54) A series of pitched notes arranged in order of height, from which melodies and harmonies can be made.

Section (p7, 35) A recognisable part of a piece of music, e.g. introduction section. Can also refer to a group of instruments, e.g. string section.

Semitone (p26, 40) Smallest music interval used in most Western music, e.g. between C and C#.

Strings (p29) Stringed musical instruments. Most commonly refers to a group of orchestral bowed instruments, e.g. violins, violas, cellos, basses.

Structure (p6, 37) The way in which a piece of music is put together. Usually created by organising or repeating different sections in a particular order. Also called 'form'.

Syncopation (p17, 36, 37) A way of changing a rhythm by making some notes sound a bit early, often so that they cross over the main beat of the music. Common in jazz, latin and pop music.

Ternary (p18) A way of organising the sections in a piece of music, so that the first section repeats after the middle section (A-B-A).

Texture (p39, 46) Layers of sound combined to make music. More layers produce a thicker texture; fewer produce a thinner texture.

Timbre (p54) Describes the different sounds or 'tone colours' produced by instruments and voices. For example, a trumpet has a very different timbre to a violin, which helps us to tell them apart.

Tone (p26, 40) Musical interval spanning two semitones.

Unison (p41) When more than one instrument or voice performs the same line of music together at the same time (uni-son = 'one sound').

Verse/strophe (p6, 27) A section of a song where the music is the same but the lyrics are different each time it is heard.

Villa-Lobos (p21) Brazilian composer (1887–1959) who used the sounds and music of his country when writing pieces.

Work song (p25) Sung to make tedious or strenuous physical jobs easier and more bearable. The rhythm of a work song will usually go with the physical actions of the worker.